Dedication

I dedicate this book to my wonderful wife Patricia; our three wonderful children Brian, Mike and Katie; and our friendly friends—Ben our very happy dog, who recently became an Angel, and Buddy, our always cheerful cat.

Thank You All!

Special Report:
Solving America's Student Loan Crisis!

The only real solution to the $1.52 Trillion debt accumulation

The President in simple terms netted out the student debt crisis from both a student and parent perspective: "They go, and they work, and they take loans, and they're borrowed up, and they can't breathe, and they get through college and the worst thing is, they go through that whole process and they don't have any job." Trump has it right, and worse than that, when the US system hurts them, our best and brightest lose hope.

Many have excoriated the Obama Administration and government and coffee-breath professors who teach nothing, for making it worse for college graduates. They all make money on the student loan program. Trump says: "You know the one program that the U.S. makes a whole lot of money with is student loans, and that's maybe the one program they shouldn't be making money with… "So, we're going to have to start a program," he said. "We're going to do something very big with loans because you have to get these people going. They really feel down and out."

Donald J. Trump is right. Yet he is the only president who has even talked about solving America's problem with rip-off loan sharks and a government that makes big money off the backs of student borrowers. Ironically, the man willing to help is hated by the very young Americans that he speaks about helping.

College graduates and those former students not fortunate enough to complete their degrees need all the help they can get to claw their way out of huge college debt. Your author as a professor and as a father understands student debt. He feels the pain of America's indebted young adults. Kelly has intellectually analyzed the plight and the torment felt by today's millennials. Besides recommending a great solution and a do-again, this book also examines other ways to solve the problem including refinancing, extending, and providing better payment plans as well as getting universities to put some skin in the game.

This book addresses the massive $1.52 Trillion student debt already on the books and it presents a boldly unique plan to assure that students with loans have a chance of success with a job in their field of study. Isn't it about time? This book tells you how it can be done. You won't be able to put this book down before you know what you can do to help those with student debt be able to afford homes and start families and live the life of real Americans and not indentured servants.

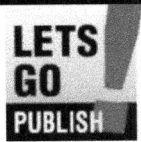

**LETS
GO
PUBLISH**

BRIAN W. KELLY

Copyright 2018 Brian W. Kelly   Editor, Brian P. Kelly
Title: Special Report: Solving America's Student Debt Crisis!   Author Brian W. Kelly
Subtitle: The only real solution to the $1.52 Trillion debt accumulation

Published by: LETS GO PUBLISH!
Publisher: Brian P. Kelly
Editor: Brian P. Kelly
P.O Box 621   Wilkes-Barre, PA   www.letsgopublish.com

Library of Congress Copyright Information Pending
Book Cover Design by Brian W. Kelly;
Editing by Brian P. Kelly

ISBN Information: The International Standard Book Number (ISBN) is a unique machine-readable identification number, which marks any book unmistakably. The ISBN is the clear standard in the book industry. 159 countries and territories are officially ISBN members. The Official ISBN For this book is also on the outside cover: **978-1-947402-65-2**

The price for this work is: **$6.95 USD**

10   9   8   7   6   5   4   3   2   1

Release Date: October 2018

LETS GO PUBLISH!

Acknowledgments

I appreciate all the help that I have received in putting this book together as well as all of my other 134 other published books.

My printed acknowledgments had become so large that book readers "complained" about going through too many pages to get to page one of the text.

And, so to permit me more flexibility, I put my acknowledgment list online, and it continues to grow. Believe it or not, it once cost about a dollar more to print each book.

Thank you and God bless you all for your help.

Please check out www.letsgopublish.com to read the latest version of my heartfelt acknowledgments updated for this book. FYI, Wily Ky Eyely loves this book and recommends it to all. Click the bottom of the Main menu on the web site!

Thank you all!

Preface:

Rarely does a book title explain exactly what a book is about. This book is the exception. This book explains in detail the rationale and the solution for solving the student loan debt crisis in America. There is no question about it.

It helps to recall that President Obama increased the National Debt by $9.1 Trillion in just eight years, hoping to assure that illegal aliens had all the resources they needed to take as many American jobs as they could. He just about doubled our debt and has nothing to show. Tell me where the money went? Are any debt-ridden college graduates doing better after Obama spent $9.1 Trillion? He could have paid off all the debt and had lots left over and America would still be prospering under Trump.

It is too bad that he did not have the foresight to use $1.52 Trillion of that wasteful largesse to help America. With less than 15% of this reckless spending, the former president could have been a folk hero among many Americans.

He could have and should have spent more wisely and wiped out 100% of the student debt now strangling our young American adults and holding the US economy hostage. Until the student debt crisis is put behind us, the most physically capable and more than likely, the brightest people in America, our recent college graduates between the ages of twenty and forty, have been taken out of the game. Poof; they are gone!

They will not be in a position to start a business, buy a home, new appliances, a new car, or begin a family. I am talking about 45 million student loan borrowers—seventy percent of all college students / graduates. At a time that we needed Obama's leadership the most, right after the sub-prime mortgage crisis when the economy was at a standstill, how could the former president have missed the opportunity to reinvigorate the economy by freeing 45 million young people from debtor's prison.

The former president had the opportunity to reinsert forty-five million Americans with a propensity to spend money into the economy and the prior president chose not to act. He chose not to free them from the shackles of repaying a massive and unfair student debt load that will keep them out of the economy for years and years to come.

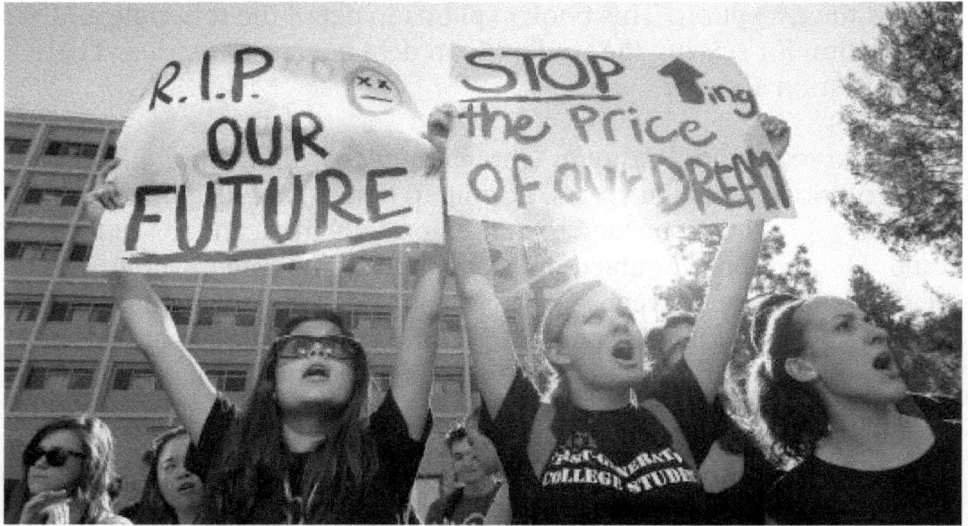

More than 1 million student loan borrowers each year go into default.

Outstanding education debt in the U.S. has tripled over the last decade and now exceeds $1.52 trillion, posing a greater burden to Americans than auto or credit card debt.

For many, the payments are proving unmanageable. By 2023, nearly 40 percent of borrowers are expected to default on their student loans. That's when a person has not made a payment toward their education debt in roughly a year, triggering it being sent to a third-party collection agency.

It has gotten so bad that within four years after leaving school, nearly a quarter of the borrowers had defaulted. Who does that help. After they default, they live in the shadows along with the illegal aliens who have taken all the types of jobs that these young Americans might have gotten.

This book tells Congress and the 45th Ppresident how to solve the crisis and it tells American that nothing happens without a vigilant population. That means we must hold our government and our politicians accountable for solving this crisis that affects almost every family in America.

More and more Americans, even those of us who have paid off all of our student debt are looking at today's student loan dilemma differently from any other group of debtors in American history. The groundswell of concern for removing so many potentially productive Americans from the economy at one time is at an all-time high with more Americans asking Washington to forgive this debt so that young Americans can engage and so that the economy can be jump-started to make all Americans successful.

Young Americans are literally choking on their student debt. It has their lives stopped and each year that it is not solved is another day in a veritable debtor's prison. It is so bad that 50% in a recent survey would be willing to give up their most fundamental freedom (voting) to be able to lead a normal life. Hopefully, it will not have to come to that.

A survey from Credible, conducted through Pollfish, hits the seriousness of the situation right on the head. It is understandable that young Americans would want a chance in life by having their debt removed. But it was surprising to many what they would be willing to do to be free of those loans. The most popular answer the 500 respondents between the ages of 18 and 34 chose for what they would be desperate enough to sacrifice was *"suffrage."* Yes, half surveyed said they would give up the ability to vote in the next two presidential elections to be able to move their lives forward.Our youngest Americans are really hurting.

It is not just those who would be set free who feel forgiving student debt is an idea whose time has come. More Americans believe that the US should forgive all federal student debt than feel that the recipients should pay their loans back. The results to many, of the survey conducted by MoneyTips.com, were shocking. Nearly 42% agreed with the statement, "I believe President Trump's Department of Education should forgive all federal student debt to help the economy."

Less than 37% disagreed, while the remaining 21% neither agreed nor disagreed. Even those who for years were pressuring Congress to do the right thing were taken back.

For example, Brandon Yahn, founder of "studentloanguy.com said: "It is surprising that the majority of the US population supports this measure…Perhaps this student debt burden has spread more across all generations, and popular sentiment is turning the corner as it relates to student debt." Perhaps it is that more than the debtor goes in the hole.

You may know that federal student loans don't require co-signers, but private student loans typically do. If the student's parents don't have good credit scores or aren't willing to co-sign, a loving grandparent often is asked to step in. The experts say that most of the time, the grandparents should say no. Because they do not say now, the loan companies have no problem garnishing their social security checks. So you can see, one default student debt and many in a given family are affected. A forgiveness may be the only solution.

When asked further about the positive impact on the economy and the impact of future student's ability to attend college in the future, most believe that this is a one and done. There should never be another forgiveness. And, so the consensus is that there needs to be a fool-proof solution for new student debt so that new high school aspirants to college do not sign up for debt when they do not need to do so.

There are a number of notions in this book besides wiping out all of the $1.52 Trillion. This book discusses many of the theories about how this happened and how it can be made to never happen again. Additionally, it discusses a number of student resources and a few tricks that are both honest and long overdue. America can not afford a full generation—its most physical and most capable generation to be wiped out of the US economy because they signed a student loan. It just isn't fair.

Why did Brian W. Kelly write this book?

Brian W. Kelly wrote this book because he cares about college graduates being able to move on with their lives. I am publishing this book because I care. This book identifies the most notable and most serious flaws in student tuition financing. It then solves them by prescribing a number of Kelly-unique solutions to help get the program back on track.

I hope you enjoy this book and I hope that it inspires you to take the individual actions necessary to help the government of the US stand firm against any attacks on democracy from outside or from within this great country. A great start of course is to stop the government's gouging of young Americans, who are plagued with student debt. Instead government should be a helpful tool in solving this deep moral and financial dilemma for our country.

I wish you the best.

Brian P. Kelly, Publisher
Wilkes-Barre, Pennsylvania

Table of Contents:

About the Author

Brian W. Kelly retired as an Assistant Professor in the Business Information Technology (BIT) program at Marywood University, where he also served as the IBM i and Midrange Systems Technical Advisor to the IT Faculty. Kelly designed, developed, and taught many college and professional courses. He continues as a contributing technical editor to a number of IT industry magazines, including "The Four Hundred" and "Four Hundred Guru," published by IT Jungle.

Kelly is a former IBM Senior Systems Engineer and IBM Mid Atlantic Area Specialist. His specialty was designing applications for customers as well as implementing advanced IBM operating systems and software facilities on their machines.

He has an active information technology consultancy. He is the author of 135 books and numerous technical articles. Kelly has been a frequent speaker at COMMON, IBM conferences, and other technical conferences.

Brian was a candidate for US Congress from Pennsylvania in 2010 and he brings a lot of experience to his writing endeavors.

Brian Kelly knows that the student debt crisis can be solved without bankrupting America.

Chapter 1 The Best Student Debt Solution

Congress and the President: need the will to act

There are many solutions for student loan debt at different levels discussed in this book. The first and the best solution is depicted in the title of author Brian Kelly's book: *Wipe Out All Student Loan Debt Now!* This book was a predecessor book to this and it has much more detail. This book is shorter and much easier to read. It gets to both the issues and the solutions much quicker than the larger book.

The ideal solution as introduced, from an American point of view, has economic ramifications that along with the new tax plan can add to a major jump re-starting of the economy. The ideal solution of course is to wipe out all of the student debt from all college loans as soon as possible and to start again. There are many ways the US can afford this and prosper because of it.

This act alone would free forty-five million debt-ridden former college students, mostly graduates to go ahead and get real lives for themselves. They will be in a position to start a business, buy a home, a new car, and begin a family.

Student loan debt is a big problem for America. Despite the big burden on the country, colleges and universities are still making a ton of money on the backs of jobless students despite not providing their end of the bargain. They continue to coax as many seventeen and eighteen-year-olds as possible to sign on the dotted line for a life of misery and massive debt. Soon 40% of the new students with loans will default, thereby removing them without big-time help, from the opportunity to participate in the American Dream

Student Debt is now the second highest consumer debt category - behind only mortgage debt - and higher than both credit cards and auto loans. Loans are being granted like as if the spigot will be shut down some day. It should be shut down. According to analysts, there are more than 45 million borrowers who collectively owe $1.52 trillion in student loan debt in the U.S. alone. The average student in the Class of 2018 has student loan debt approaching $50,000 with many at the $100,000 level. Graduate students check in with debt of $200,000 to $500,000.

The negative impact of so many student borrowers is clear. Essentially, the US has 45 million Americans, who are putting a big chunk of their monthly income towards their student debts. That means that they aren't spending on other economy-boosting goods or services. This group also has less money to save, invest, or even start a business. The burden is so heavy that over 10 million (and growing) have stopped paying a dime. This phenomenon is called being in default.

I am not the only person who thinks it is a good idea to start over again on student loans and wipe what we have off the books as soon as possible. There are countless articles on the Internet with more and more being written everyday of Americans pushing for a solution so that we can re-enfranchise a lost generation of Americans. It is long overdue that the Congress and the President should solve this huge problem for America.

David Muccigrosso, an Armchair Economist, blogging at //www.quora.com, on Feb 12, 2013 took a shot at answering this important question in his article titled: *What would be the economic impact of forgiving all US student loan debt?*

Back on January 29, 2009, Robert Applebaum at http://studentdebtcrisis.org wrote a similar piece. He reminds us that in 2009, President Obama signed into law a $787 billion stimulus package on top of Bush's grossly mismanaged $700 billion TARP bailout from September. That, by the way is more than the total student debt of today, $1.52 trillion.

Applebaum notes that shortly thereafter in 2009, the Federal Reserve basically printed an additional $1,000,000,000,000 to inject more funds into the monetary system, undoubtedly having the effect of diminishing the purchasing power of the dollar. Now, we are approaching twice the total of all the student debt. In other words, if we acted then to forgive the debt, it would be all gone, and all paid for.

Since then, the US government has paid out trillions of dollars in additional bailouts, handouts, loans and giveaways, with no end in sight as our leaders tried to do anything and everything to get our spiraling economy under control. While some of what Washington has already done may act to stimulate the economy, much of the trillions of dollars already spent will, no doubt, has proven to be just money wasted.

Freeing 45 million young adults so that they can participate in the economy would not be a waste. It would bring about a major economic boom.

Instead of funneling billions, if not trillions of additional dollars to banks, financial institutions, insurance companies and other institutions of greed that are responsible for the current economic crisis, why is it not a better idea to allow educated, hardworking, middle-class Americans to get something in return? After all, they're our tax dollars too!

Forgiving student loan debt would have an immediate stimulating effect on the economy. With Trump, we are already back to 4.2% GDP growth. Who knows what having 45 million ready-to-spend, millennials reengaged in the economy will do for the country?

Responsible people who did nothing other than pursue a higher education would have hundreds, if not thousands of extra dollars per month to spend, fueling the economy right now.

Those extra dollars being pumped into the economy would have a multiplying effect, unlike many of the provisions of the 2009 era stimulus packages. As a result, tax revenues would go up, the credit markets would unfreeze, and many jobs would be created. Consumer spending accounts for over two thirds of the entire U.S. economy and in 2009, consumer spending declined at alarming, unprecedented rates. Therefore, it stands to reason that the fastest way to revive our economy quickly is to do something drastic to get consumers to spend.

This proposal would quickly revitalize the housing market, the ailing automobile industry, travel and tourism, durable goods and countless other sectors of the economy because the very people who sustain those sectors will automatically have hundreds or, in some cases, thousands of extra dollars per month to spend.

Given the economic climate inherited from the Obama years, as well as the plans to spend trillions of additional dollars that have been in the works, one must wonder what is so objectionable about giving a real helping hand to real people with real struggles.

In 2009, the then new Obama Administration was supposed to be about change. Yet, nothing in the economic stimulus package represented a significant departure from the way Washington has always operated – it was merely a different set of priorities on a higher scale, but it's certainly not materially different from any other economic stimulus package passed during the past few decades.

More Americans Want to Forgive Trillion-Dollar Student Loan Debt Than Want It Repaid

MoneyTips http://www.ajc.com
4:00 p.m. Friday, July 21, 2017 Business and Money news

More Americans believe that we should forgive all federal student debt than feel that the recipients should pay their loans back. In a shocking survey recently conducted by MoneyTips.com, nearly 42% agreed with the statement, I believe President Trump's Department of Education should forgive all federal student debt to help the economy. Less than 37% disagreed, while the remaining 21% neither agreed nor disagreed.

"It is surprising that the majority of the US population supports this measure," says Brandon Yahn, Founder of studentloansguy.com. "Perhaps this student debt burden has spread more across all generations, and popular sentiment is turning the corner as it relates to student debt."

...

While income wasn't a factor, gender seemed to affect people's feelings on this subject, with more women favoring forgiveness over men. 47% of the women agreed or strongly agreed with the statement, while less than 36% of the men felt the same way.

...

Reasoned millennial money expert Stefanie O'Connell, "Women are now more likely than men to get a college degree, which may explain why they would favor student loan forgiveness at higher rates. They're also likely to experience career interruptions due to childbearing and caretaking, which can impede their lifetime earning potential and, consequently, their ability to pay back their loans.

Finally, many of the lucrative jobs that don't require a college degree tend to be in male-dominated fields - carpentry, electrical, etc. - which might explain why more women favor loan forgiveness."

...

Says Student Loan Hero, expert Miranda Marquit, "Many millennials, who thought they were doing the right thing, took on student loan debt only to graduate to an economy where jobs have been scarce, and wages have been mostly stagnant for decades. Gone are the days when you could work for the summer and pay for the following school year. Check tuition rates. They more available student loans have been, the more colleges and universities have raised tuition.

As a society, we sold a dream and failed to deliver. You can make payments on your loans for decades and barely make headway." Adds Marquit,

"As a result, these millennials are unable to help the economy in other ways. Research indicates they are putting off financial milestones that come with economy-building benefits.

"All the consumption that comes with things like buying homes and starting families is being lost because the largest generation yet doesn't have money to spare. Student loan forgiveness would go a long way toward helping millennials feel stable enough to take the next steps in their financial lives, as well as even starting businesses."

Keep thinking about it and then one day, let's just do it!

Chapter 2 No Problem Is Without a Solution

The government is not your friend

Despite self-serving governmental, political, and academic apologists suggesting that there is no real student debt crisis, just ask a recent millennial graduate when they hope to start a family. You better have a lot of time. We keep hearing about a student debt crisis. Yet, politicians continue to argue that there is no student debt crisis though everybody else knows that there is. Perhaps the definition of a crisis can tell us--*a time of intense difficulty, trouble, or danger.*

The fact is that recent students with major loans are having trouble paying them back. Everybody in America knows that. The fact is that the young adults in our country have put off major life plans until their personal crisis improves from hopeless to manageable.

Is the country in crisis? Whether the country is in crisis or not, taxpayers are now on the hook for about $1.52 trillion outstanding in student debt. That makes student debt substantially larger even than credit card debt. Moreover, it's not looking like it's going to get any better in the future. The graduating class of 2017 owed an average of over $37,000, up from less than $30,000 in 2014. We're moving quickly to indebtedness at the $50,000 level.

The real problem is many problems

The people that say there is not a student debt crisis suggest that most people will repay their debts though it may take them 10 to 20 years to do it. The real problem, these people believe is the expanding default rate on student loans. Just a couple years ago, the defaulters were at 7 million. Now 10 million no longer pay a dime of their loan back. Most simply cannot.

Think about another ticking time bomb. The biological clock on graduates cannot wait until the debt is paid. Time will run out, especially with students graduating at 22 to 24 years of age. One child families may very well become a common phenomenon.

Your friendly US Department of Education produced a report recently that noted the two-year cohort default rate on student loans increased from 9.1% for FY 2010 to 10% for FY 2011 In 2017, the default rate has already climbed to 11.2% and the average monthly out of pocket student loan payment for a borrower aged 20 to 30 years is $351. They make less money than their parents so the monthly outlay for those that can repay anything takes its toll. That is a good part of a mortgage payment or a nice payment on a family car.

It cannot be argued that more student debtors are falling behind on their federal student loans. The share of Americans at least 31 days late on loans from the U.S. Department of Education ticked up to 18.8 percent as of June 30, up again from the same time last year.

The total in US student loan debt has climbed to $1.52 Trillion and as of right now, about 45 million Americans have some student loan debt.

Most experts say the program is operating in crisis mode.

Who's to blame?

The easiest people to blame for these problems are, of course, the students. After all they are the ones who took out the loans. However, like your dad and my dad would say, "What do they know?" That's actually the problem.

For some reason, which I admit has little merit, we here in the US have decided that the norm for every child born in America is to have a college education. Consequently, I would suspect we have the worst electricians, plumbers, and auto mechanics in the world as we basically shut down the technical skills education once taught in high school.

From what I have observed, the richest guys in many towns today run the plumbing businesses, electrical businesses, and of course body shops and vehicle repair shops. My cousin Frank, who is a great guy by the way, made his millions in New Jersey by being the one body shop in his home town. Now, he makes a few bucks in a different way. He bought about 300 acres in a PA county town that is producing fracking oil in a big way.

Guys like cousin Frank are tickled that many of their future competitors opt to get college degrees. It follows that when they have to pay off the loans for those degrees, they will not have the cash to build a new garage in town to compete against cousin Frank. That may help Frank, but it does not help America.

The supposed plusses of having to have a degree, for years has convinced the vast majority of US high schools to dedicate their efforts to getting their students prepared for a college education. With so many in America possessing four-year degrees today, the sheepskin is often worth little more than the cost of the ink and the parchment.

Think about the gal or guy who sat next to you in a number of high school classes. Were they college material? When everybody, regardless of smarts became college material, colleges figured out how to bolster their income by admitting them on probations that could continue for four years. They do not graduate but their loans become due when they walk out of the school without a return pass.

So, there are many students who put in their four years without being fully admitted and are then kicked out without a degree when it is obvious that they had taken enough courses to prove that they never should have gone to college. Now, these poor souls cannot find enough money to start a landscaping business, so they get a job flipping hamburgers trying to come up with $350 a month or more to pay off their four-year student loan. Is that a crisis? It sure is.

Somebody in a university and some coffee-breath faculty advisor, who knows colleges are in it for the money, helped convince Johnny or Janie that they could make it in college, whether they should have the smarts for a degree or not.

Consequently, forty-six percent of those who start college, dropout before graduating. As hard as it is to believe, one of the major reasons for this is undoubtedly the fact that they should never have been admitted to any self-respecting college in the first place. Every college is expanding. They are becoming big businesses and the ease of seventeen and eighteen-year-olds getting a big loan help grow their big businesses.

Though we think their mission is to educate, even non-profits want to make a lot of money to give to their faculty and staff. We may forget sometimes that colleges are a business and businesses must survive by having customers who can pay their bills. How wonderful for these institutions with no hearts, that Johnny and Janie equally are able to get guaranteed student loans. How nice it is that colleges are assured of receiving their full tuition even if neither student had a chance for success.

Another part of the problem is that most seventeen and eighteen-year old's have mush brains and they use valedictorians as models when they are trying to eke out a C in Gym class. Yes, all valedictorians will graduate from college unless they rig the game against themselves. But, most high school students sporting a C average ought to try to find a job as a beautician if they have dexterity, or a barber, or an auto mechanic. If they can get into plumbing or become electrical apprentices, their lives are set.

In across the country, the McDonalds and Burger King guys get their $15.00 hourly wage, then the fully degreed sociology majors who are out working in kindness industries, will be able to up their salaries by about $10,000 and they can then take over the jobs these non-degreed personnel have. Not only can these college grads flip the burgers better in most cases, they can also handle the cash register.

Additionally, management may find a great brain among them and bring them in to a corporate program. So, why the degree and why the student loan for sociology or psychology if a student is not headed for a PhD or an MD.

High school 17 and 18-year-old seniors, though they "know everything," are simply not prepared to choose the right college majors so they pick one that is easy. Since they have "I know everything," cards printed by their buddies in Print Shop or elsewhere to present to anybody offering counsel, it is tough to talk them out of a career in rocket science. After a year, when they flunk out of rocket science, they can always switch to Sociology, and pick up their D average so they can graduate with a big "C." For businesses, interviewing a C average college graduate candidate, the C stands for "can't do the job." They know that such students would not be good bookkeepers.

Sociology is the most altruistic major as the graduate gives to others all her life and she makes little more than the horse groomer at the end of town, who never spent a dime to get a degree. Nonetheless, there are other degrees similar to sociology that millennials are encouraged to pursue. For example, many choose majors that align with their passions such as film and video arts, pre-school education, psychology, anthropology, archaeology, fine arts and music. It's great work if you can get it.

Like sociology, the pursuit of knowledge in these majors might be fun and rewarding but it rarely leads to a well-paying career. For that matter, many of the young people who choose these types of careers won't even be able to find jobs. In fact, as of March 2012, 60% of college graduates were unable to find work in their fields of study.

I have seen statistics that suggest that about 80% of college graduates have no choice but to return to the roost and let mom and dad continue paying their big bills in life. No wonder the Democrats think we need illegal aliens to do the jobs in America that Americans never trained themselves to do well.

Colleges and universities are big culprits in the student loan crisis

It is an understatement to suggest that colleges and universities are at least partially to blame for the student debt problem, especially the for-profit schools. Whether they admit it or not, all colleges and universities other than the finest of the well-endowed, are in a competitive business.

Please permit me to tell you a secret that is not such a secret in the boardrooms of our country's most successful universities. It is as clear as day when you follow the prospects of students who matriculate after much consideration. They contemplate whether they should be greeting card designers or plumbers or college graduates.

While they are in such deep thought, a great number of them are enticed by local high school counselors with affinities to certain colleges or by various program counsellors in universities that need students to enroll in various programs to assure institutional revenue. To get the revenue, the counsellors present loan packages that the prospective students cannot ever afford even with a degree in the art of leisure. That is the first reason why there are so many loan defaults.

Traditional 50 and 100-year old colleges and/or universities that would be classified as non-profit endowment based institutions, are more likely to tell the truth to a high-school flunky, who thinks he should go to college. The flunky wants to go to college often because the girlfriend is going to the same college. Many otherwise bad future marriages would be on the verge of collapse today if the admirer was not already rejected by the institution for lack of cranial substance.

Not all traditional non-profit colleges are so appropriate as to actually deny admittance to a poor scholar. *For-profit* colleges and universities are the worst at grubbing for money from the young chump who wants to be a college graduate because his girlfriend is smart enough to be admitted.

Under the covers, *For-profits'* admissions departments are run as marketing departments. Marketing to students nobody else wants is their mission. The loan amount and the loan default rates are the highest at these institutions of higher-priced learning. When they default, American taxpayers are again left holding the debt bag, even though the institution is private.

As an example, students that borrow similar amounts to pay for their schooling end up defaulting at a much higher rate at for-profit institutions. In fact, 26% of for-profit students that took out loans between $5000 in $10,000 ended up defaulting versus the 10% of students at community colleges that defaulted and the 7% at four-year traditional schools.

Private schools are not immune to this either. They, too, must compete for students. The more aid they can offer prospective students, the more they will attract. This puts pressure on them to accept "marginal" students and for their financial aid offices to promote federal student loans as a way to pay for their educations. Yes, Virginia, federal student loans must be repaid.

Yet, I have not seen any academic institution in any of the categories from traditional to for-profit ever suggest that the huge assets of the major academies and the lesser capabilities of the lesser endowed, should join together to help the poor students, who tried in their institutions but failed. There are no rescue pans for them. All of their profits are their profits and they choose to use no profits to help their failed products, their graduates, get through the loan costs needed to have a little chance in life.

Maybe we should remind Academia that they are not supposed to be profit making snobs. Their mission is the education of young adults.

The federal government

As hard as it is to believe for those of us that think the federal government can do no wrong, the hoity toity constabulary running all the important agencies in Washington DC have had no problem in ripping-off millennials who managed to get their degrees. They again have had no problem bamboozling those who have put in a lot of years, taken a lot of subsidies, and still have not graduated. And, of course, the piece de resistance is that many of the products of these institutions have yet to get their first job.

It is even more clear that the federal government itself has played a major part in creating the student debt crisis. The government in Washington likes to wash itself clean of any wrong-doing but as a modern-day comedienne would say quite astutely: "They're Bad, Bad, Bad!"

The *don't be a plumber mentality* has not only helped fuel the idea that everyone should have a college education, it has also made it very easy to get student loans. The socialistic government of the Obama years especially encouraged every high school senior, via their guidance counselors, to fill out and submit the Free Application for Federal Student Aid (FAFSA). This assured that colleges got paid for attendance regardless of the quality of the student or the quality of the education.

The form they fill out not only goes to the Department of Education (Ed), it goes to every school for which a student has applied. The process then becomes automatic as the federal credo is "nobody should be denied an opportunity to fail in college."

Sometime in late spring each student receives a notice of the federal financial aid they will receive based on their family's financial situation. In most cases a large part of this aid will be in the form of federal student loans, which the average family will have a very difficult time not taking. It looks like free money when it is not due for four years hence.

It cost nothing for Joey to go to college. But, when Joey graduates the debt machine begins asking to be paid. If Joey does not finish college, the debt machine comes after Joey and his family even harder because they know unless Joey gets a job, nobody will be paying back their loan.

Some say that not even a Chapter 7 bankruptcy can help if you have no money

Suppose, independent of your college life, you were reckless, and you ran up $40,000 in credit card and medical debts. The government of the US permits you to be able to get this debt discharged through a method called Chapter 7 bankruptcy.

Why is this? Nobody's perfect and many Americans mess up and find themselves being enticed to engage in debts which they can never repay. Often the seller of the good or service is part of the perpetration. After a while, when an individual realizes he or she cannot get out of the hole they dug for themselves, the government offers them relief.

This type of bankruptcy is known as personal bankruptcy. It is a last resort for people who are so far under, they would be candidates for the poorhouse if there was one that would take them. There is another form of bankruptcy called Chapter 13. Both Chapter 7 & Chapter 13 personal bankruptcy can eliminate overwhelming debt. With Chapter 13, you are put on a payment program so all debt will be paid for in three to five years. With Chapter 7, depending on the finding, you may find all debts discharged.

Debts may include credit card debt, bank loans, medical bills, most court judgments, and deficiencies on repossessed vehicles. Bankruptcy is not free as there is almost always a competent lawyer involved who wants to be paid. The lawyer has to figure out whether to take on a client and he or she must assure the firm can get paid. Not all lawyers will take on all cases. You will have to pay the law firm up front.

Using Chapter 7 bankruptcy, a debtor will almost always have to pay all attorney fees before your case is filed. In many cases, a friend or relative makes that payment. With Chapter 13, a large percentage is paid up front and the law firm gets paid the rest over three to five years as payments are made to all creditors.

As one might expect, an individual debtor is subjected to major harassment by debt collectors and even garnishment of wages. Those former students who are living paycheck to paycheck and have defaulted on some of their student loans are typically greeted every day with ten or more phone calls from the crack of dawn until the end of the day.

Stop Harassment / Garnishment

It is nice for an individual debtor to receive some relief from such a major disruption in their lives. For example, by law, most actions against a debtor must cease once a Chapter 7 or Chapter 13 personal bankruptcy has been filed. Creditors cannot initiate or continue lawsuits, wage garnishments, or even telephone calls demanding payments.

Keep Assets / Rebuild Credit

Debtors may be able to keep their cars, primary residence, and certain other personal belongings when filing for Chapter 7 or Chapter 13 personal bankruptcy. In Chapter 7, non-essential personal items are sold to help pay for the creditors losses.

Personal bankruptcy law firms are needed because they have the skills to help debtors retain their assets and show them what steps they must take following the bankruptcy so that the debtor can quickly get back on their feet. They also help in rebuilding the debtor's credit immediately after the bankruptcy is resolved.

There is nothing that prevents a debtor, once free of poor-house level debt, to choose to voluntarily pay back creditors without the burden of harassment or garnishment.

Why did the Congress feel it necessary to write bankruptcy legislation? Debtors who are unable to pay their debts do not pay their debts. That is a fact. They may never get credit for anything in their lives again but there is no fallacious debtor's prison where they are kept until debt is repaid.

Nearly two centuries ago, the United States formally abolished the incarceration of people who failed to pay off debts. Bankruptcy laws actually help creditors collect when the individual has non-essential assets. However, regarding debtors, the clear purpose of Chapter 7 bankruptcy is to discharge certain debts to give an honest individual debtor a "fresh start." The debtor has no liability for discharged debts.

This form of bankruptcy can get almost all unsecured debts discharged except for alimony, spousal support, child support and... student loan debts. As tough as Congress is on student loans, they are easy on everyone else as debtors Only kids with the intelligence or experience to say no to college can go through bankruptcy.

In other words, if your debt is your college education, the Congress has made it law that you must work all your life to pay off that debt. If you had big gambling debts, they would be forgiven by bankruptcy. Yes, for smart kids without a nickel in their pocket, and a huge student loan, this is hard to believe.

Chapter 3 Is the Student Loan Game Rigged?

Do Colleges and Universities have an unfair advantage?

You bet they do!

It costs Academic Institutions nothing when students come out sacked with a lifetime of debt after four to six years with no jobs. Donald Trump can recognize a rigged game better than any man in America. He can sniff them out and call them out and /or play against them and still win. He thinks the student loan game is rigged against students and it favors the universities and the government disguised as loan sharks.

Trump does not like that the student loan game is rigged, and he has promised to fix it. The President believes that universities must have some skin in the game for any long-term solutions to be built.

My best friend since college, Dennis Grimes has an unbeatable way to solve the problem in the future to assure that colleges are more selective about whom they cosign regarding their ability to complete the degree of their choice. President Trump will like the Grimes Plan This plan is presented in the last chapter and you will enjoy it. You'll be saying that Grimes is a sharpy! And you will be right. It is a great solution to add university skin in the game and solve the problem for the future.

Many people are affected by the crisis and, so it is a topic at the dinner table in many homes—especially in those homes in which the student loan invoices are beginning to arrive from junior's or missy's four-to-siz-year past sojourn into campus life.

When people in the US discuss the student debt crisis, most focus on how it affects them personally. If they are not directly affected, they discuss the rapid growth in outstanding debt and its impact on the economy and the country.

They may also discuss some of the recent milestones, which are not very positive. For example, student loan debt exceeded credit card debt in 2010 and it exceeded auto loan debt in 2011. It is rapidly rising, and it passed the $1 trillion mark in 2012. It is currently at about $1.52 trillion and growing.

It is a big problem. The Wall Street Journal recently reported that More than 40% of student loan borrowers are either in default, delinquency or have postponed repaying their student loans. It is a crisis and having the federal government making over $45 billion off the backs of student borrowers via excessive interest payments does nothing to help matters. Obama needed these billions to fund Obamacare.

With about 40% of students defaulting on their loan paybacks—mostly because the payments are so large, is a problem for all America. It is also a big disgrace for a country that does not want to be labeled as "Third World."

These milestones don't tell us much about the impact of all that debt on the students themselves. Seventeen and Eighteen-year-olds are making lifetime decisions even today with little counselling other than "Don't Worry! Be Happy!"

These naïve high school seniors were originally told by a friendly high school counsellor or a college financial aid officer or both that everybody borrows, and it is a privilege to be able to attend this college with the help of the university's quality loan package.

Does that sound familiar. If Joe's Hot Car Lot was scamming young adults at the same rate as academia, the Justice Department would shut them down. At least Joe's Hot Cars can make it around the block. What about the kids with $50,000 in debt, no degree, and no job?

Sometimes as learned by default interviews, there was never an up-front discussion of the loan impact when it came time to repay it. As hard as it is to believe, the loans came so easy that 53% of the students when graduating, did not even know there was a payback. And we all know what payback is!

70% of all college students have borrowed and many who are already enrolled still have more to borrow before they finish their degrees and then have to pay for their college education. It is a national travesty.

America and Americans had been told by Team Obama until 2017, that America is not exceptional. The way government treats the best and the brightest, who owe huge amounts of school debt, is proof that this past president and his administration were not kidding.

Meanwhile, the past president put the government in charge of huge chunks of the student loan industry. Team Obama picked up over 40 $billion a year in profits by scobbing students with high government interest rates when they put Sallie Mae out of business.

No matter how immune you get to hearing about government $billions here and there, remember that a $billion is an extremely large amount of money. Even a $million is quite large. A $million is so big it gives more meaning to the word billion. It is 1000 million. Would you not like to have a $million right now?

Obama's government made the debt problem even worse for student loan debtors by taking more interest dollars than needed to sustain the program. Uncle Sam is on track to make $66 billion in profits after Uncle Obama took over the student loan program six years ago. That's why Donald Trump wants to turn the program back over to private enterprise at competitive rates. Why should students in default status be providing financial support for Obamacare?

With inflation, a college degree isn't worth much anymore. Everybody has one and the ones who should not have been admitted in the first place, are jobless and in debt up to their ears. Often, they are marginal students and they have two to six more courses to go when they are forced to drop out with an almost "C" average.

Some suggest, and I agree that certain college majors ought not ever be granted loans. Professionals with sociology and philosophy degrees and C averages are not in demand. Do you know anybody who is employed as a philosopher?

Today, many students opt to continue after graduation to pursue a Master's degree. Universities, knowing the depleted value of their undergraduate degrees suggest that students take out more loans and get a Master's Degree. which may give them a better shot at a job or a promotion--maybe. It may also make them postpone a family until they are into their fifties. Something is not right.

After five years or so, experience counts the most. IBM paid for my MBA, but it did not help me one way or another in my career. However, it did give me the minimum credentials to teach as a professor in a college, which I did for over thirty years part time, adjunct, and then "full-time" for a bunch of years.

I know from my own family that students with graduate degrees have substantially higher debt. Law School graduates for example, often owe about $200,000 and MD Degrees owe as much as $500,000. If most undergraduate students were getting high paying jobs as in the past, the problem would not be as severe as they would be able to pay back their loans. It is enough to make many students lose hope.

Bartenders, Waiters, and Short Order Cooks have a tough time handling the new Obama government approved repayment rates for their undergraduate debt. Ironically, a college education is one of the few things in life that's value is going down, while its price is going up.

More and more parents are advising their less than valedictorian-level children to think about a trade or a less-skilled job, before committing a zillion dollars to a debt they may not ever be able to pay back.

Why is student debt increasing? Government under Democrat control with grants and support for postsecondary education has simply chosen not to keep pace with increases in college costs. Democrats have sold out American-born college students to gain the favor of the coffee-breath liberal professors in the universities and foreign national graduates who are about to overstay.

In many ways, liberal professors talk students out of being productive members of society. Look what is happening at once prestigious universities across the country. Tell again what a free-speech zone is.

Government money, AKA Santa Claus, that could have been used to help parents and students with this massive debt, has been diverted to welfare programs and other schemes that give Democrats advantages over American students . The one-time party of the people has forgotten completely about Americans, who are now saddled with huge debt repayment plans while foreign students who overstay their visas are getting their jobs simply by accepting lower wages.

Colleges are oblivious as nothing has hurt them. They make a ton of money while students and graduates scrounge for alms. This is their renaissance period as we find them going about like their product has no issues.

Chapter 4: Solving the Student Loan Crisis and the Housing Crisis

Young people are kept down by Universities

Young and old borrowers alike owe collectively 1.52 trillion dollars of debt from their public and private student loans. With the bad economy for so long, as much as 30% of the borrowers are defaulting on their loans and this number is rising every year.

The former students simply cannot make the minimum payment. It is so bad that older students with loans are now turning 62 years of age. They get an unexpected, unwelcome surprise when their social security checks begin to be garnished by the government loan shylocks to pay off these old loans.

It is worse than you can imagine. My research discovered an 82-year old gentleman who once guaranteed a friend's loan and he is now paying 40% of his social security check to pay off the loan. He is left with $750 per month. Can this be America? Yes, it is, and in his case and many others, the principal was paid off long ago. The Obama rates for student loans are so high, Obama could not pay them.

Many, including me, a guy who has been a professor, teaching at colleges for over 35 years, are questioning the value of a university education. It is not a good situation when loan brokers get to collect the student cosigned debt from government's social security payments that are given in order to sustain life.

Our major topic in this book is student debt and how to get rid of it for good. Yet, more and more experts are concluding that there is a tie-in of student loan debt and the lack of a robust housing business in the US. The home ownership rate in the United States has been at a 50-year low. As you might expect, it is not admissions counsellors but economists and realtors who worry about that.

The National Association of Realtors and ASA recently found that 71 percent of student loan borrowers who did not own a home cited their college loans as the main prohibitive factor. More than half indicated that they expect their student debt to delay their home purchase by five years or perhaps even more. Housing starts are a great leading indicator for the economy and when the most likely age group, twenty to forty-year-olds are not able to afford mortgage payments, something has got to change. That's why I wrote this book.

Record high home prices certainly don't help matters either. Student debt and the market aren't the only reasons millennials put off home ownership. They are not sure of a lot of things and, so they marry and have kids later in life than prior generations did. Additionally, they have seen higher unemployment rates and more sluggish wage growth than in the past. "All of that is postponing the entry point of home ownership," said Lawrence Yun, NAR chief economist.

Should we worry? Yun thinks we should. He says, "First-time buyers cause a chain reaction" in the housing market, which creates activity throughout the economy, from moving truck rentals to appliance purchases.

"That demand is central to the health of the broader real estate market," said Jonathan Spader, senior research associate at Harvard's Joint Center for Housing Studies. People are most likely to form a family and enter the housing market for the first time in their 20s or 30s. And when young adults buy their first home — often a lower-priced starter — it allows an established household to sell. "To the extent that there's weak demand at the first-time home-buyer level, it prevents existing homeowners from trading up," Spader said.

Student loan debt creates obstacles to home ownership in a few different ways. "The first is the drag on income," Spader said. It makes it tough to accumulate a down payment.

Another reason is that a student loan can make it harder to qualify for a mortgage. Lenders want all of your monthly debt obligations, including your potential mortgage payment, to make up no more than 43 percent of your monthly income. If you already pay 14 percent or more of your income toward a student loan that doesn't leave much room for a mortgage.

Another big problem on the horizon is that 11.1 percent of student loans are at least 90 days delinquent — more than any other type of consumer debt. "The impact of those defaults on the credit reports could be a barrier to home ownership in the future," Spader said. "A default is a really big deal -- it's the equivalent of a bankruptcy or a lien on your credit report,"

Asked what college hopefuls should consider as they compare schools and financial aid offers, experts suggest that it's critical to understand what your monthly loan bill will be after graduation. "Students and consumers see a number of $40,000 or $100,000, and that number is hard to wrap their heads around." The big question is "Is a $1,000 a month payment or more, every month, really going to be OK for you?"

There are a lot of possible remedies to the student loan crisis out there, which will help the homeowner crisis, but there are no guarantees. Other than wiping out all student debt and beginning again, there is no silver bullet.

When people can't get jobs, and don't have the resources to pursue the dreams of a sustainable life in America, then they get to this situation where the divide between the haves and have-nots gets wider. It ripples all across our culture and economy.

That's why the overriding recommendation in this book is for the government to address the problem; find the assets to afford it and wipe out all student debt in one big whoosh! I can assure you that there will be no housing crisis once millennials are spending-enabled. Homeowners will be everywhere if we can just get the debt noose off the backs of millennials.

Looking at the student side again, it is intuitive that students in the bottom 60% of the class have substantially lower prospects for work in their chosen field than the top 40%. One after another, many debtors in the bottom 60, are wishing they could have a do-over on that loan decision they made at 17 or 18 years of age. If so, most would never bite that bad apple again.

They now know that their huge loans; many over $100,000 are beginning to ruin their lives. Nobody, from the high-school counsellors to the College admission officers offered counselling on student debt and the negative impact it would have on the lives of so many of our young in America. Over 70% of graduates are on the hook to pay off student loans. If government, especially our Congress, was not one of the perpetrators, this would already be declared a national emergency?

Where are the good jobs that were promised by the universities for all the money borrowed? At the same time that most graduates cannot get jobs, the jobs they do get, pay less and are often not in their field of study. The average salary of college graduates has gone down 10% in the past few years while inflation is growing at an ever-faster clip.

Moreover, 85% of college graduates from 2011 have had to swallow their pride and move home with mom and dad because they could not afford life on their own. It doesn't take a rocket scientist to call out: "Houston, we have a problem!"

The problem, to repeat, in addition to our finest representatives, is caused by coffee-breath professors, former coffee-breath professors serving as administrators, government stoolies, politicians, and progressive Democrats that like it when Americans are dependent on government.

Meanwhile the media is not saying anything bad about the universities that permit more and more foreign students into their programs. When the foreign students graduate, they are supposed to surrender their student visas, and head home. But, they do not. Moreover, the US government does not track them to make sure they do go home when their time is up in America. It makes it tough for Americans to get jobs.

Life is so good here in America, that foreign graduates often prefer to become illegal aliens, as nothing bad ever happens to an illegal alien anymore. The bad things happen to American students who graduate and get no jobs.

Buying a home without a job?

With more and more former students not being able to survive without their parents, the student debt crisis also has an impact on the student borrower's ability to ever break away. Purchasing a home is out of the question as the college loan is already bigger than the graduate's mortgage for a first home should be.

As noted, this is already having a major effect on the US housing market and it will continue for years to come. Who will buy the new homes if not the young Americans, hoping to begin families.

No solution is simple. With about 30% or more former students ultimately defaulting on their loans, and many more trapped in a financial abyss from which they can never escape, Congress can certainly create a better way to help the student borrower, the housing market, and the taxpayer, all at the same time.

Considering that in the 2009 crisis, with all of the gifts from the federal government to corporations and banks that were failing, many experts have written that this money would have been better applied to the student-debt crisis. Once relieved from the staggering debt under which they suffer, you can bet millennials, all 45 million of them free from the shackles of unending debt, would be out there making America great again by purchasing one needed item after another.

I would suggest that Congress assure that in times when savings earns just a percent or two in interest, student lenders have their interest rates capped at something that is well out of the usury category. Former collegians with loans are in crisis mode in their lives while protected lenders never had it so good.

Congress can do much better for all Americans. I am a conservative and some say Republicans would not go along with a forgiveness of the student debt burden on the only Americans positioned to spend a ton of money if they had it. Shame on Republicans as many Trump loyalists have been saying for years.

Whether Congress takes it out of the fed system as it did in the $3 trillion 2009 major bailouts to corporations and banks, and nobody missed it, or it authorizes President Trump to sell some assets that are helping nobody in America, to pay for the economic restoration, the Congress has enough sheckles to forgive all student loans if they wish.

If the Congress sits on its duff and wrings its hands, the next major action for those hands that I would recommend would be that they clutch the steering wheel of the family car as the one-time so and so's from such and such go back to such and such, never ever again to return to Washington DC. Good bye!.

Can you imagine the major spark in the economy if all of a sudden, millennials became the big spenders and were enabled to throw house parties in homes they never thought they could afford?

The fact that Obama's government made about $43 Billion and more per year by charging higher than reasonable interest rates on student loans shows that solving the debt problem was never a priority during the eight years before the current president. Let's hope Mr. Trump looks past Obama to create a system that works.

Chapter 6 Forgive all Student Debt & Pay off the National Debt

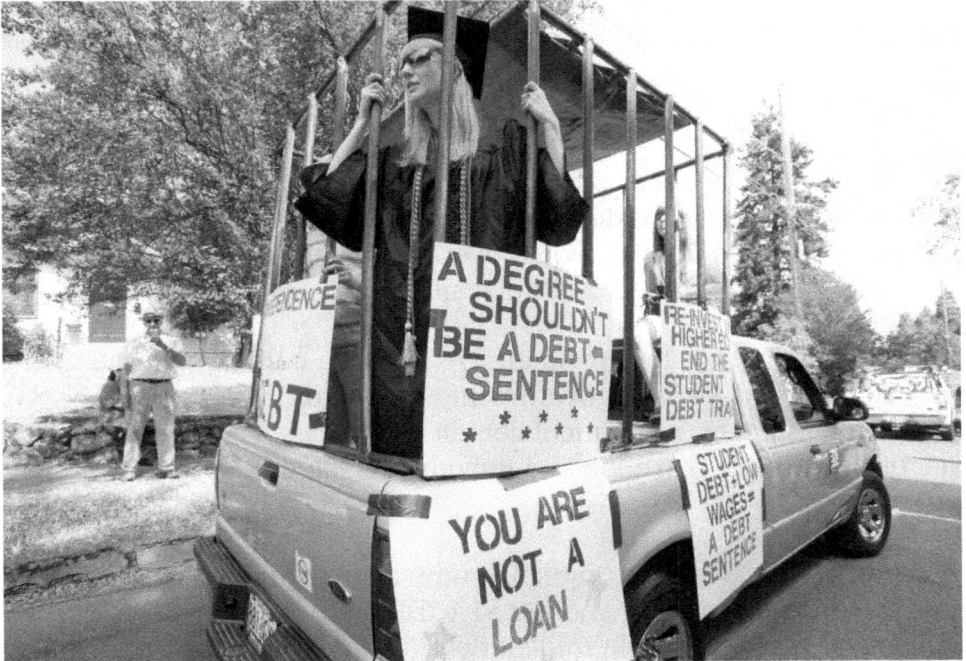

Piggyback on a President Trump plan to eliminate the National Debt.

America is a rich country. We have learned our lesson on student debt and on the National Debt. We have more than enough assets to wipe them both out and start fresh with a new set of rules to assure this never happens again. Only those who can afford to pay back student loans should get them, and each budget must be balanced 100%. No more US national credit card. Yes, Virginia, it is that simple.

As a candidate, now President Donald Trump promised that he would balance the national budget and pay off the national debt. By studying different thoughts on the matter, I am convinced that President Trump is right.

In no scenario am I talking about destroying Yosemite or the major National parks in the country. That would not be popular with anybody. But if we want to, we can set our debt clean in such a way that all Americans would be helped. On December 4, 2017, the president listened to Utah and gave them back about 2 million acres that Obama had stolen from them. By making selective moves such as this, we can position US and/or states assets to help America and Americans, rather than sit there doing nothing for anybody.

Keeping everything nice, a lot of minerals can produce a lot of what is needed to pay off the Student Loan Debt. Show me a reason why millennials should not be favored over monuments in which even bicycles are not permitted? Isn't that silly?

President Trump is a businessman. He has been considering selling off $16 trillion worth of U.S. government assets in order to fulfill his pledge to eliminate the national debt in eight years. He simply has to sell of a little over $1 trillion and nobody will have student debt anymore.

A senior adviser with the original Trump campaign Barry Bennett said. "How about adding another $1.3 trillion to the [national debt] repayment plans to handle student debt?" Why is that not a bad idea?

Even though the new total is $1.52 trillion, I could not agree more. Why should our next generation of intellectuals be the ones who are hurt the most by government? Once we get it paid off, we must get more selective as to who gets loans as we begin to Americanize America. We cannot ever let student loans get out of hand again.

Donald Trump is quoted as saying: "The United States government owns more real estate than anybody else, more land than anybody else, and more energy than anybody else," Bennett announced. "We can get rid of government buildings we're not using; we can extract the energy from government lands, and we can do all kinds of things to extract value from the assets that we hold."

Why should Americans be unable to begin their lives when the US is sitting on such massive assets. The bad newspapers such as the Washington Post and the New York Times want the world to think that our President is a buffoon. He is not. He is just not part of their swamp. That says it all.

In a wide-ranging interview with The Washington Post, Trump said he would get rid of the $19 trillion national debt "over a period of eight years." Of course, the debt now is approaching $21 trillion. Check out the debt clock to find out how fast our inept Congress can spend your money. http://www.usdebtclock.org/

I believe Donald Trump knows what he is talking about!

Chapter 7 Eliminate All Student Debt!!!

Student debt is huge

We have already heard the cries of young American chained to their student loans. All Americans must want to solve this national crisis. College graduates with massive debt cannot buy homes, and furniture or new cars, and they cannot get married and begin families.

Can America afford to lose a whole generation of offspring. America and Americans can do a lot better than this for our newest generation of young adults.

In 2018, the total amount of student debt outstanding is $1.52 Trillion. More and more young adults simply cannot repay. Most are looking for relief but do not want to put the rest of America on the hook for an education that went bad for them. Universities and colleges take no blame--though many Americans see them as the real perpetrators.

If Academia admitted the truth—that they lied to incoming freshman, then maybe everybody today owing the national government for a student-loan package that committed kids to pay and pay and pay and pay and gain nothing, would be asking Academia to pony up a few bucks to help solve the student debt crisis.

Some citizens and many of our friends have asked: "Why do our young people no longer matter?" Do they matter? To Congress, they do not matter at all.

We Americans live in an age when everybody seems to have a reason to pick on millennials. It happens this group owes most of the student debt in America. I am sure your average Bank Officer would not consider loaning a "spoiled" millennial "ingrate" as much as a dollar for a cup of coffee.

However, the same Bank Officer just a few years previous, would OK a millennial for a hundred-thousand-dollar loan or more so they could attend a college or university. Why is that? They loaned huge sums even though the young faces of the borrowers gave away the fact that they had yet to finish with puberty.

I regret that is true and now many of our youngest citizens are stuck because they committed to debt at 18 years of age and some even as young as seventeen. They may have even signed their loan papers at sixteen. Should these young people have been entrusted with such huge loans? You intrinsically know the answer.

Whether millennials are deserving of the bad rap or not, they represent a lost generation of our society. For the sake of all of America, they need to be invited back in to society. We all have student loan debtors in our families – sons, daughters, nephews, nieces, even grandparents and parents—when we consider cosigners in the indebted mix.

We admire those who have been able to pay their own loan debt, but we acknowledge many in our own families who cannot afford even the interest. And, so they feel they have no choice but to become leaches on society and as time passes, we see that they no longer even have the will to participate in the loan game at all.

They default and hide from the collectors and they have little to spend on anything. This hurts these young people more than you can imagine and it also hurts our economy as they should be the biggest spenders.

I have proposed that any candidate for national office offers legislation when first elected to make sure we solve this nasty American problem. There have been many other debt-reliefs in our history but none that could deliver such an immediate positive punch to so many actual Americans all at once.

The upside would be overwhelming. It would be a giant humanitarian return and a major economic return—far greater than any bailout in history. Let's consider it. It is not unprecedented.

A Bailout is a Bailout?

Many of us remember bailouts of the past from 2007 pre-Obama onward. We had bank bailouts, auto company bailouts, TARP bailouts and many other unnamed bailouts. Did any of these help your family? Of course not. Help with student loans would help regular Americans more than any of these bailouts.

Bailout fever began right before Obama became President and continued. The President managed all of the money—trillions. He chose not to give a dime to help student loan debt but spared no expense showering the degenerate financial institutions that owned his candidacy—with gold.

Mike Collins, a Forbes Magazine contributor whose expertise focuses on manufacturing and government policy had this to say:

"Most people think that the big bank bailout was the $700 billion that the treasury department used to save the banks during the financial crash in September of 2008. But this is a long way from the truth because the bailout--[ten years later] is still ongoing".

"The Special Inspector General for TARP's summary of the bailout says that the total commitment of government is $16.8 trillion dollars with $4.6 trillion already paid out." FYI, that is three to ten times the total amount of student debt owed today.

The same banks are now larger and still "too big to fail." But the indebted students are small potatoes, not significant enough to care about. So, their loans must be repaid with no government assistance.

"But it isn't just the government bailout money that tells the story of the bailout. This is also a story about lies, cheating, and a multi-faceted corruption, which was often criminal."

Like most elements of his presidency, Obama made the situation worse when he commandeered the student loan program from Sallie Mae and other lenders. The government now pulls in more than $50 billion a year from charging usury level interest rates to student borrowers. The Obama Student Loan Company charges 6.8% as student interest rates.

The CBO estimates that the interest rate on these loans could quickly be reduced from 6.8 percent to 5.3 percent if Obama had not earmarked the profit from the backs of students to subsidize Obamacare.

Not only were millennials duped into huge college loans when they were so young that Clearasil was one of their major expenses, they were duped into believing Obama was in their corner.

Despite what a number of my conservative friends believe, your author believes these student victims deserve a break. Many are now adults. Many of the Americans stuck with huge cosign tabs are grandparents on Social Security. The government actually garnishes their SSR "checks" to pay back the Obama loans.

The federal government is putting up $16.8 trillion dollars as of 2018 for big banks, and other nameless faces receiving bailout dollars. We still do not know who is getting our money. But, we do know that at about $1.48 trillion of student debt in total in 2018, the crony friends of government are receiving ten times more of a benefit than our children. Granted many of our children do not need a dime but a much larger percentage need much more than a dime! America and Americans can do a lot better for this generation.

Students are still being victimized by usury after being preyed on as 17-year-olds by admissions counsellors for an all-but worthless college education leading to no job. If given the choice would you be helping the big banks, or would you ask the government to help our own kids?

What do the people think about Student Debt?

Four in ten Americans believe that President Trump's administration should forgive all federal student debt in order to help stimulate the economy, according to a reasonably new survey revealed in 2017. As time goes by as more Americans realize we are excluding a full generation of Americans in our economy, this number will increase from a simple majority to an overwhelming endorsement of wiping out this scurrilous unfair debt as soon as possible.

We should bring these 48 million former students back into the American way of life as soon as possible.

As we indicated at the beginning of this chapter, the largest share of blame for the student debt crisis lies with the promises made by over-zealous admissions counsellors who convinced immature adolescents to accept a new paradigm about growing up in America. Big bully adults told them it is OK at 18 or 17 or perhaps even 16, to sign up for $100,000 loans. We now know that for this generation, that was bad advice.

No American can want a full generation of other Americans to be left behind in the Trump economy. We need this debt eradicated now and we need to install safeguards so that young kids who think that they can handle anything, do not have to learn that they actually cannot by experiencing this tragic lesson. Without some help from other Americans, it is hopeless.

According to MoneyTips.com, attitudes have changed from a time when Americans thought college students should be punished for making bad choices to today, when we need 48 million new spenders in our economy. Can you imagine the positive economic impact if they were all unleashed at the same time?

They would be unleashed into a world of productivity if no longer burdened with this massive debt. Many of us know first-hand the consequences of this debt burden. Though millennials may not be the most gracious in asking for help, they are Americans, not DACA immigrants, and they need our help now. Even if your child got through himself or herself, without any help, could you dare say no?

Do you want these young people to be poor all of their lives? Are you mad at them because they cannot pay back their loan but not upset with others who use the bankruptcy courts or the welfare system to handle their debt? Think about the answer, please?

The raw economic fact, regardless of your philosophical preference is that spenders with the greatest potential to spend today are not spending at all in real numbers because of student debt. They are not getting married. They are not having families and they are not buying homes. We must solve this scourge on our country so that this generation can produce other generations of reasonably wealthy regular Americans.

I have friends who say: "my Johnnie and my Elsie had to pay it all off and they did…those lazy louts should just cough it up!" As a country, the US has not ever had to vote to permit the poor to starve because somebody paid something more or less than somebody else. We should not start now.

Just remember that the children of Americans, our children are not MS-13 members in disguise; they are our kids—American kids. They were snookered to join academia for what they were deceived into believing was an indispensable college degree by depraved loan sharks. Let's give them a full chance to recover.

After what they went through, why not another chance? It costs a university nothing when their students with huge loans fail. They make millions on student loans. Please let that sink in. Should they also take a stake at helping bring these students that they simply cast away, back as productive human beings?

Let me review the plight of young American college attendees and graduates. Barely out of adolescence, these young Americans were wheedled into commitments based on fraudulent promises by high school admissions counselors in their junior and senior years as well as financial institutions whose risk is mitigated by the government.

It is unfair to pit experienced loan sharks against adolescent teenagers. The students were further damned by a paid-for Congress, whose lobbyists insisted that these select few, with student debt, distinct from all of the others in debt in America, should have no opportunity for any relief in the bankruptcy courts. Why is that?

Non-college graduates with a trillion dollars in credit card debt are still able to obtain full relief from the courts. Why did Congress exclude these former teenagers, who clearly have been the biggest victims of loan-shark organized racketeering ever seen in America? Why?

We need to take action to eliminate all student debt. I hope you all agree. Let's help these young Americans before they are lost forever. And more importantly let's fix this broken system so this cannot happen again.

Young teenagers were told all through high school that the best ticket for a successful life is a college education. Is this true today? The salaries of college graduates recently began to lag behind those of non-college educated professionals such as plumbers, electricians, computer repair personnel, operating engineers, and more. Worse than that, graduates do not get jobs in their majors because most of the jobs are taken by graduates from other countries with special visas--who frequently overstay.

Because of their reliance on these deliberately false misrepresentations, each of these young Americans now owe an approximate average of $50,000 in student debt while their admissions counsellors and loan sharks owe nothing. Instead, they revel in riches, in their Mercedes, BMW's, and third vacation home on the lake.

Unscrupulous malefactors with self-interest-filled agendas persuaded America's teenagers, many so young they still had Acne vulgaris, to dig themselves huge financial holes with no escape. Universities are at least partly responsible for their unfulfilled promises. Don't you think?

We must also consider what liability universities may share in compensating this lost generation where one out of six student borrowers must default today—a figure that only has increased and will increase more with time.

Removing this debt may not fully compensate for the bad hand they were dealt, but its consequent increase in economic activity will benefit all of us. It will boost the US economy beyond expectations. We are already giving bailouts of over $16 trillion to obscenely rich people in corporate shadows. Who says we cannot help our American progeny even if they are millennials?

Right now, we need a mere 10% of that number to pay for the write-off of student debt without hurting taxpayers and without putting any banks under. The savings over three years, for example from implementing a resident visa program alone would pay off the entire student debt that exists today. Why support illegal aliens when we can help Americans?

One last point. It helps to recall that President Obama increased the National Debt by $9.1 Trillion in just eight years, hoping to assure that illegal aliens had all the resources they needed to take as many American jobs as they could. Name me a better reason?

This is six times the amount of debt owed by young Americans. Obama nearly doubled our debt. And what do we have to show for that? For a typical college student in the Obama years, the answer is frankly... nothing. By contrast, debt relief for our young Americans will be visibly positive in its impact.

So, let's say Congress and the President together wipe out all student debt because it is the fair thing to do. How do we prevent this from ever happening again? For this tremendous answer, I thank my great friend, Dennis Grimes whose solution combines some skin in the game for Academic Institutions to the mix and thus assures that no student will ever carry debt unless the student is successful with a job in their field of study. Here is how the new loan system designed by Dennis Grimes would work.

Nobody gets a loan unless the college or university agrees to take all of the risk of the loan. This is the key differentiator. If the student is successful, she or he will pay very reasonable amounts on a monthly basis until the loan is repaid. If the student is jobless, since the university vouched for the student, the school will owe all of the debt.

Academic institutions are smart. They will stop lending quickly to students with very little prospects of being able to pay the loan back. If students do not maintain acceptable averages, they will be expelled post haste, and the university will pay their balance. If the same student wants to go to college in the future, it will be cash only. What do you think? Thank you Dennis. It is simple and perfect.

A Rigged System

You and I are confident that President Trump would re-enfranchise America's youngest generation of adults. by eradicating student debt and paying the balance via savings no longer spent subsidizing illegal immigrants.

In his own words, regarding recent graduates: "They go, and they work, and they take loans, and they're borrowed up, and they can't breathe, and they get through college and the worst thing is, they go through that whole process and they don't have any job." President Trump has it right. He sees how this rigged system has snuffed out the optimism of a bright generation that now gives way to cynicism and despair.

I am expecting that every candidate for office in 2018 already knows how important this is. I would expect any candidate to help enact the legislation that eradicates all student debt, effective immediately. As a side benefit for the candidate, there are 48 million former students plus cosigners and family, who would immediately have an affinity for any legislator who proposed this solution.

The people realize that none of this will more than likely not happen until we can get new legislators in Congress and the US Senate. Then, these measures can be brought up to the Congress of the US and will become well-known to the conservative press, seniors and millennials. Any American saddled today with the direct result of the abuse of our legislators should not be quiet in these important matters. Remember Congress at the ballot box.

God Bless America!

Other Books by Brian W. Kelly: (amazon.com, and Kindle)

Millennials Say America Was "Never That Great": Too many pleased days of political chumps not over!
White People Are Bad! Bad! Bad! In 2018, too many people find race as a non-equalizer.
It's Time for The John Doe Party… Don't you think? By By Elephants.
Great Players in Florida Gators Football… Tim Tebow and a ton of other great players
Great Coaches in Florida Gators Football… The best coaches in Gator history.
The Constitution by Hamilton, Jefferson, Madison, et al. The Real Constitution
The Constitution Companion. Will help you learn and understand the Constitution
Great Coaches in Clemson Football The best Clemson Coaches right to Dabo Swinney
Great Players in Clemson Football The best Clemson players in history
Winning Back America. America's been stolen and can be won back completely
The Founding of America… Great book to pick up a lot of great facts
Defeating America's Career Politicians. The scoundrels need to go.
Midnight Mass by Jack Lammers… You remember what it was like Great story
The Bike by Jack Lammers… Great heartwarming Story by Jack
Wipe Out All Student Loan Debt--Now! Watch the economy go boom!
No Free Lunch Pay Back Welfare! Why not pay it back?
Deport All Millennials Now!!! Why they deserve to be deported and/or saved
DELETE the EPA, Please! The worst decisions to hurt America
Taxation Without Representation 4th Edition Should we throw the TEA overboard again?
Four Great Political Essays by Thomas Dawson
Top Ten Political Books for 2018… Cliffnotes Version of 10 Political Books
Top Six Patriotic Books for 2018… Cliffnotes version of 6 Patriotic Boosk
Why Trump Got Elected!.. It's great to hear about a great milestone in America!
The Day the Free Press Died. Corrupt Press Lives on!
Solved (Immigration) The best solutions for 2018
Solved II (Obamacare, Social Security, Student Debt) Check it out; They're solved.
Great Moments in Pittsburgh Steelers Football... Six Super Bowls and more.
Great Players in Pittsburgh Steelers Football ,,,Chuck Noll, Bill Cowher, Mike Tomin, etc.
Great Coaches in New England Patriots Football,,, Bill Belichick the one and only plus others
Great Players in New England Patriots Football… Tom Brady, Drew Bledsoe et al.
Great Coaches in Philadelphia Eagles Football..Andy Reid, Doug Pederson & Lots more
Great Players in Philadelphia Eagles Football Great players such as Sonny Jurgenson
Great Coaches in Syracuse Football All the greats including Ben Schwartzwalder
Great Players in Syracuse Football. Highlights best players such as Jim Brown & Donovan McNabb
Millennials are People Too !!! Give US millennials help to live American Dream
Brian Kelly for the United States Senate from PA: Fresh Face for US Senate
The Candidate's Bible. Don't pray for your campaign without this bible
Rush Limbaugh's Platform for Americans… Rush will love it
Sean Hannity's Platform for Americans… Sean will love it
Donald Trump's New Platform for Americans. Make Trump unbeatable in 2020
Tariffs Are Good for America! One of the best tools a president can have
Great Coaches in Pittsburgh Steelers Football Sixteen of the best coaches ever to coach in pro football.
Great Moments in New England Patriots Football Great football moments from Boston to New England
Great Moments in Philadelphia Eagles Football. The best from the Eagles from the beginning of football.
Great Moments in Syracuse Football The great moments, coaches & players in Syracuse Football
Boost Social Security Now! Hey Buddy Can You Spare a Dime?
The Birth of American Football. From the first college game in 1869 to the last Super Bowl
Obamacare: A One-Line Repeal Congress must get this done.
A Wilkes-Barre Christmas Story A wonderful town makes Christmas all the better
A Boy, A Bike, A Train, and a Christmas Miracle A Christmas story that will melt your heart
Pay-to-Go   America-First Immigration Fix
Legalizing Illegal Aliens Via Resident Visas Americans-first plan saves $Trillions. Learn how!
60 Million Illegal Aliens in America!!! A simple, America-first solution.
The Bill of Rights By Founder James Madison Refresh your knowledge of the specific rights for all
Great Players in Army Football Great Army Football played by great players..
Great Coaches in Army Football Army's coaches are all great.
Great Moments in Army Football Army Football at its best.
Great Moments in Florida Gators Football Gators Football from the start. This is the book.
Great Moments in Clemson Football CU Football at its best. This is the book.
Great Moments in Florida Gators Football Gators Football from the start. This is the book.
The Constitution Companion. A Guide to Reading and Comprehending the Constitution

The Constitution by Hamilton, Jefferson, & Madison – Big type and in English
PATERNO: The Dark Days After Win # 409. Sky began to fall within days of win # 409.
JoePa 409 Victories: Say No More! Winningest Division I-A football coach ever
American College Football: The Beginning From before day one football was played.
Great Coaches in Alabama Football Challenging the coaches of every other program!
Great Coaches in Penn State Football the Best Coaches in PSU's football program
Great Players in Penn State Football The best players in PSU's football program
Great Players in Notre Dame Football The best players in ND's football program
Great Coaches in Notre Dame Football The best coaches in any football program
Great Players in Alabama Football from Quarterbacks to offensive Linemen Greats!
Great Moments in Alabama Football AU Football from the start. This is the book.
Great Moments in Penn State Football PSU Football, start--games, coaches, players,
Great Moments in Notre Dame Football ND Football, start, games, coaches, players
Cross Country with the Parents A great trip from East Coast to West with the kids
Seniors, Social Security & the Minimum Wage. Things seniors need to know.
How to Write Your First Book and Publish It with CreateSpace. You too can be an author.
The US Immigration Fix--It's all in here. Finally, an answer.
I had a Dream IBM Could be #1 Again The title is self-explanatory
WineDiets.Com Presents The Wine Diet Learn how to lose weight while having fun.
Wilkes-Barre, PA; Return to Glory Wilkes-Barre City's return to glory
Geoffrey Parsons' Epoch... The Land of Fair Play Better than the original.
The Bill of Rights 4 Dummmies! This is the best book to learn about your rights.
Sol Bloom's Epoch ...Story of the Constitution The best book to learn the Constitution
America 4 Dummmies! All Americans should read to learn about this great country.
The Electoral College 4 Dummmies! How does it really work?
The All-Everything Machine Story about IBM's finest computer server.
ThankYou IBM! This book explains how IBM was beaten in the computer marketplace by neophytes

Amazon.com/author/brianwkelly
Brian W. Kelly has written 177 books. Thank you for buying this one.

www.ingramcontent.com/pod-product-compliance
Lightning Source LLC
Chambersburg PA
CBHW070943280326
41934CB00009B/1994